W9-BCY-084

Marine Firefighters

by Meish Goldish

Consultant: Douglas B. Dillon
United States Coast Guard (retired)
Executive Director, Tri-state Maritime Safety Association
Chief, Maritime Incident Response Team
Camden, New Jersey

BEARPORT
PUBLISHING

New York, New York

Credits

Cover and Title Page, © Siri Stafford/Thinkstock, © Carabay/Fotolia, and © Horizon International Images Limited/Alamy; 4, © Kieran Carley; 5, © Mary Altaffer/Press Association; 6, © William Van Dorp; 7, © Mary Altaffer/Press Association; 8L, © Zuma Press/Alamy; 8R, © Radius/Superstock; 9, © Peter Santini/U.S. Navy; 10T, © Fox Photos/Stringer/Getty Images; 10B, © Mario Burger/Burger International Photography; 11, © Bloomberg/Getty Images; 12–13, © Britt Crosby; 14, © Henry Ray Abrams/Getty Images; 15, © Britt Crosby; 16–17, © Edouard H.R. Gluck/Press Association; 17, © U.S. Army Corps of Engineers from USA; 18–19, © Handout/Reuters/Corbis; 20–21, © Najlah Feanny-Hicks/Corbis; 21, © USN/Alamy; 22, © USN/Alamy; 23, © USN/Navy; 24, © Jared Soares; 25L, © AlamyCelebrity/Alamy; 25R, © U.S. Naval Research Laboratory; 26, © Britt Crosby; 27, © Peter Stehlik; 28TL, © Mario Burger/Burger International Photography; 28TR, © Greg Bishop; 28BL, © Mario Burger/Burger International Photography; 28BR, © Joshua Sherurcij; 29L, © wavebreakmedia/Shutterstock; 29R, © Flashon Studio/Shutterstock; 31, © Rick Whitacre/Shutterstock.

Publisher: Kenn Goin
Senior Editor: Joyce Tavolacci
Creative Director: Spencer Brinker
Design: Emma Randall
Photo Researcher: Ruby Tuesday Books

Library of Congress Cataloging-in-Publication Data

Goldish, Meish.
  Marine firefighters / by Meish Goldish.
    pages cm. — (Fire fight! The bravest)
  Includes bibliographical references and index.
  Audience: Ages 7–12.
  ISBN-13: 978-1-62724-098-7 (library binding)
  ISBN-10: 1-62724-098-5 (library binding)
  1. Ships—Fires and fire prevention—Juvenile literature. 2. Harbors—Fires and fire prevention—Juvenile literature. 3.
Fireboats—Juvenile literature. I. Title.
  VK1258.G65 2014
  623.88'8—dc23

                                2013034721

For more information, write to Bearport Publishing Company, Inc., 45 West 21st Street, Suite 3B, New York, New York 10010. Printed in the United States of America.

10 9 8 7 6 5 4 3 2 1

Contents

Fire Below Deck!

It was a warm Saturday afternoon in New York City on July 14, 2012. About 500 people had come to shop at **Pier** 17. The waterfront mall is located at the South Street Seaport next to the East River. Suddenly, a fire broke out under the pier's large wooden **deck**. Thick black smoke quickly filled the air.

The Pier 17 fire was caused by faulty electrical wires under the deck.

The frightened crowd rushed to escape the smoky area. Within minutes, firefighters arrived at the pier. They jumped from their trucks and began to try to put out the blaze underneath the deck. Unfortunately, their hoses weren't long enough to reach the raging flames. How could the fire be **extinguished**? This was a job for **marine** firefighters!

Marine firefighters often use boats instead of trucks to fight fires and rescue people.

FDNY (Fire Department of New York) marine firefighters approaching the blaze at Pier 17 from the East River

Heroes on the Water

After receiving an **emergency** call, marine firefighters sped to Pier 17 in their **fireboats**. By the time they arrived, the fire had spread about 100 feet (30.5 m) under the deck. The wooden deck crackled from the **intense** heat of the flames. The firefighters knew they had to act fast to put out the growing blaze.

From their boat on the river, marine firefighters were in the best position to spray water on the flames.

To reach the fire, a group of firefighters on land used **chainsaws** to cut eight large holes in the pier's thick deck. Then, from a fireboat, marine firefighters sprayed water down through the holes to get at the flames below. Within 90 minutes, the fire was extinguished. Thanks to the brave firefighters, no one was hurt.

Firefighters on land joined marine firefighters to help battle the blaze.

A total of 145 firefighters, from both land and marine fire **units**, helped fight the Pier 17 blaze.

Becoming a Marine Firefighter

Marine firefighters, such as the ones that saved Pier 17, are trained to handle any kind of emergency in or near water. However, to become a marine firefighter, a person must first become a land firefighter. Both jobs involve battling blazes and performing daring rescues.

Whether on land or at sea, firefighters are taught how to search for and rescue a person during a fire or other emergency.

During training, firefighters practice wearing heavy gear and carrying bulky equipment.

Firefighter **trainees** go to a special school to learn how fires start and spread and the best way to put them out. They are also taught how to find and rescue people from burning buildings or other dangerous situations. After several months of training, a person may then take a course in marine firefighting. Trainees are taught how to use their firefighting and rescuing skills in or near water and on ships. They also learn how to use one of the best tools marine firefighters have—fireboats.

Marine firefighter trainees aboard a ship for a training session

Marine firefighter trainees must learn to fight fires on board several types of ships. Each ship can have different kinds of dangers. For example, a tanker ship may carry **flammable** oil.

All Aboard!

Marine firefighters depend on fireboats to help them battle waterfront blazes. The earliest fireboats date back to the 1700s. They were small boats with hand-operated **pumps** that sprayed water. Today's fireboats are cutting-edge machines. They have powerful pumps and hoses with special **nozzles** that direct the spray of the water. They are sometimes called floating fire trucks!

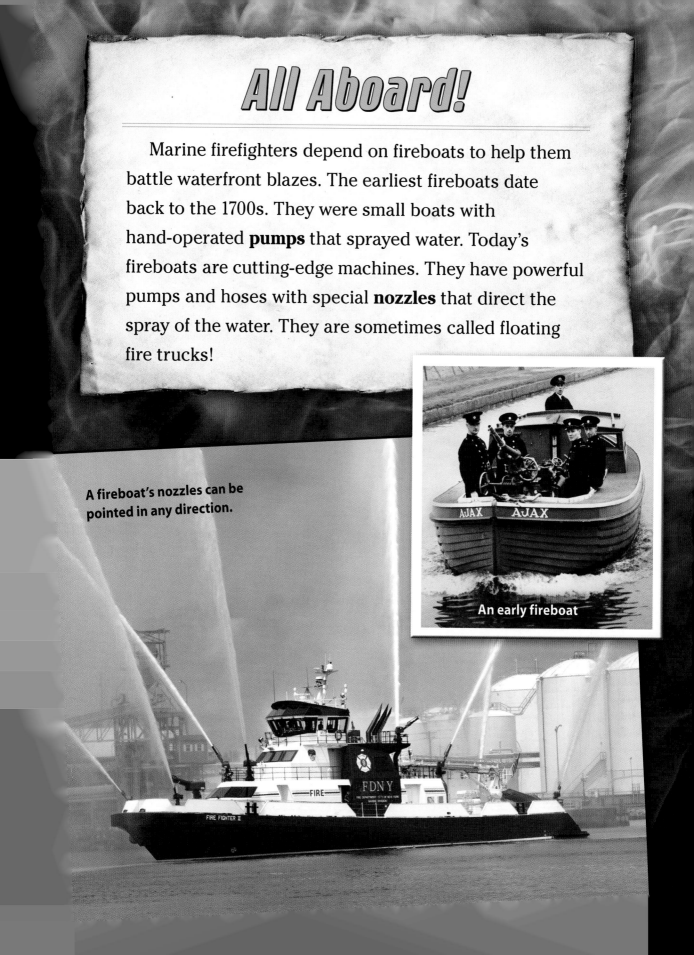

A fireboat's nozzles can be pointed in any direction.

An early fireboat

Fireboats come in all sizes. Some bigger fireboats can pump 38,000 gallons (143,846 l) of water a minute. That's twice as much water as the average swimming pool holds! To reach towering flames, the boats can shoot water up to 400 feet (122 m) in the air. That helps marine firefighters when they are battling a large fire at a waterfront building or on a ship.

Firefighters on fireboats have an endless supply of water to use. They pump it from the river, lake, or **harbor** where the boats sit.

The Los Angeles fireboat *Warner L. Lawrence* can shoot water hundreds of feet into the air.

Marine Firefighting Companies

Fireboats are kept at special **docks** or **marinas** in cities and towns. Marine firefighters may be based at firehouses near where the fireboats are docked. This allows them to quickly reach their boats in an emergency. The firefighters work in units, often called companies, led by a **battalion** chief. The chief tells the firefighters what to do and which boats and equipment to use.

NAVY YARD

A group of the FDNY's fireboats at the Brooklyn Navy Yard

F.D.N.Y.

9
8
7

Marine firefighting companies are usually part of a town's or city's fire department. Some towns and most large **coastal** cities, such as New York, Boston, Los Angeles, and Miami, have marine firefighting units. Because of its huge coastal area, New York City has one of the biggest units, including several fireboats ready to battle a blaze at a moment's notice.

The crew of *Fire Fighter II*, a fireboat based in New York City

FIRE FIGHTER II

Most marine fire companies in the United States are made up of **volunteers**.

Help on 9/11

One famous New York City fireboat served marine firefighters for more than 70 years. Members of the FDNY used the boat *Fire Fighter* to battle dozens of blazes. One of the most devastating took place on September 11, 2001. On that day, the Twin Towers of New York City's World Trade Center caught fire and fell after **terrorists** attacked them.

Black smoke poured from the Twin Towers after the attacks.

After the towers collapsed, fiery **debris** covered the ground. Firefighters on land, however, couldn't put out the flames. They had no water to spray on the fires since the water pipes and fire hydrants in the streets had been destroyed when the towers fell. Instead, firefighters attached their hoses to the nozzles of *Fire Fighter*, which was docked nearby. For five days straight, the boat pumped water to help control the fires.

Along with *Fire Fighter* (left), two other fireboats—*John D. McKean* (right) and *John J. Harvey*—pumped water on the debris after the 9/11 attacks.

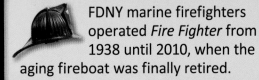 FDNY marine firefighters operated *Fire Fighter* from 1938 until 2010, when the aging fireboat was finally retired.

Rescue on the Hudson

Often, marine firefighters are called upon to perform daring rescues. On January 15, 2009, New York City's Marine 1 firefighting company took part in an especially brave rescue. The rescue took place after an airplane with 155 people on board made an emergency landing in the Hudson River.

C.B. "Sully" Sullenberger, the pilot of U.S. Airways Flight 1549, was forced to land in the Hudson River after a flock of geese flew into the plane's engines and damaged them.

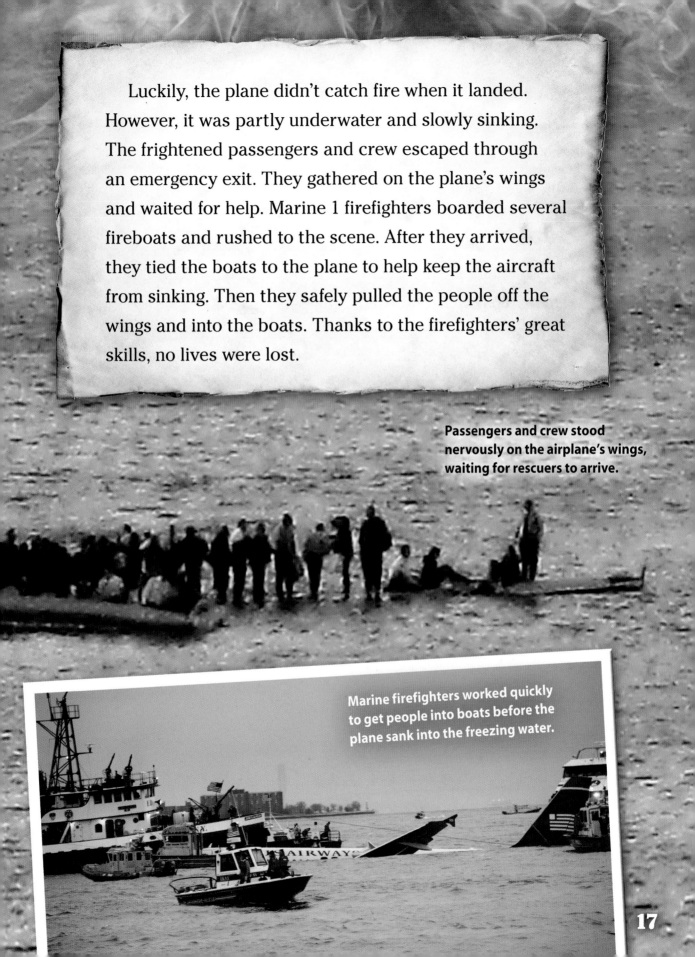

Luckily, the plane didn't catch fire when it landed. However, it was partly underwater and slowly sinking. The frightened passengers and crew escaped through an emergency exit. They gathered on the plane's wings and waited for help. Marine 1 firefighters boarded several fireboats and rushed to the scene. After they arrived, they tied the boats to the plane to help keep the aircraft from sinking. Then they safely pulled the people off the wings and into the boats. Thanks to the firefighters' great skills, no lives were lost.

Passengers and crew stood nervously on the airplane's wings, waiting for rescuers to arrive.

Marine firefighters worked quickly to get people into boats before the plane sank into the freezing water.

Explosion at Sea

Sometimes, marine firefighters battle blazes in the middle of the ocean. In April 2010, an **oil rig** called the Deepwater Horizon exploded in the Gulf of Mexico. The explosion cracked an oil pipe, sending more than 200 million gallons (757 million l) of oil gushing into the Gulf. The explosion also started a huge fire. Its flames shot high into the air and spread along the rig's platform.

Firefighting crews arrived to battle the giant blaze. They sprayed thousands of gallons of water onto the flames. However, despite their best efforts, the powerful fire could not be put out. It burned out of control for a day and a half. Finally, the flaming rig collapsed and sank into the sea.

Crews pumped water from the Gulf of Mexico and sprayed it on the fire.

Most of the 126 oil rig workers escaped from the Deepwater Horizon in lifeboats. Sadly, 11 of them were never found after the blast.

Ships Ablaze

One of the hardest kinds of blazes to battle is a fire on a ship. Why? If the ship is at sea, hundreds of miles from land, firefighters on fireboats are usually too far away to help. That's why some members of the ship's crew are specially trained to fight the fire entirely by themselves.

Fireboats fight a fire on the oil tanker, *Mega Borg,* in the middle of the Gulf of Mexico.

The firefighting team must be able to act fast to protect the ship's crew and passengers. They must also work to keep the ship from sinking. They have to move quickly up and down narrow stairs and ladders to reach the blaze. Often, they have to squeeze into tight spaces to put out fires. Sometimes, the crew has to climb down into the lower part of the ship in smoky blackness to battle the dangerous flames.

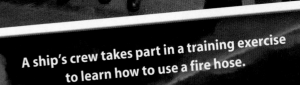

A ship's crew takes part in a training exercise to learn how to use a fire hose.

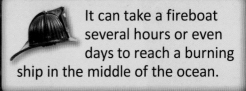

It can take a fireboat several hours or even days to reach a burning ship in the middle of the ocean.

Ship Fire Training

As part of their training, ship firefighters study every part of their **vessel**. They must know the locations of all rooms, exits, and air vents where smoke and flames can travel. To fight fire, the crew uses fire hoses, **portable** extinguishers, and fire axes that are stored on the ship. They wear special masks and carry tanks of oxygen in order to breathe clean air in hot, smoky areas.

U.S. Navy sailors learn how to put out smaller ship fires with a portable extinguisher.

The firefighting crew works in teams. They practice quickly moving hoses and other fire equipment from one area to another. Teams are taught how to pump water off the ship while hosing the fire. That way, the ship won't sink from the weight of all the water that's been sprayed on it.

A ship's crew is taught how to battle different kinds of fires. For example, an oil fire must be put out with special firefighting foam, since water may not extinguish the flames.

Ship firefighter trainees work together to move long hoses during a smoky fire.

The Newest Marine Firefighter

Ship firefighters need all the help they can get when battling a blaze. Fortunately, the U.S. Navy is designing a new robot to assist them. It's called ASH. The name stands for **Autonomous** Shipboard **Humanoid**. ASH will help firefighters put out fires more quickly, as well as battle blazes too dangerous for human firefighters to approach.

ASH is modeled after a person. It can walk

The human-like robot is designed to work independently as it battles blazes. It has a special camera that can see through dark smoke. It can walk up and down a ship's ladders and narrow stairways to reach the fire. It can even throw a special bomb filled with chemicals that help put out flames. ASH can also follow a person's voice commands and hand signals as it looks for the source of the fire.

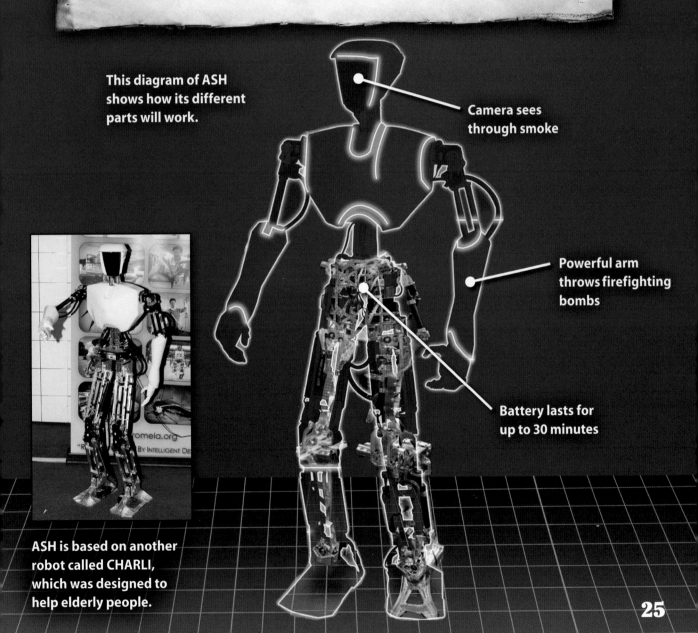

This diagram of ASH shows how its different parts will work.

Camera sees through smoke

Powerful arm throws firefighting bombs

Battery lasts for up to 30 minutes

ASH is based on another robot called CHARLI, which was designed to help elderly people.

Bigger and Better

Along with robots, today's marine firefighters are being aided by bigger and better fireboats. Recently, the FDNY received several new fireboats. One of them, *Fire Fighter II*, is 140 feet (43 m) long. That's nearly half the length of a football field!

Fire Fighter II is one of the most powerful water-pumping fireboats in the world.

Fire Fighter II can protect firefighters during terrorist attacks that make the air unsafe to breathe. The boat has a sealed **cabin** with **air filters** where the crew can breathe clean air and work in safety.

Fire Fighter II can pump 50,000 gallons (189,271 l) of water a minute. The boat also has special cameras attached to a **crane**. They allow the crew to **monitor** a fire up close. With modern equipment like this, marine firefighters can continue doing their bravest and best work.

One of the FDNY's other new fireboats, *Three Forty Three*, is named for the number of firefighters that the department lost at the World Trade Center site on September 11, 2001.

Marine Firefighters' Gear

Marine firefighters use lots of different equipment to fight fires on or near water.

A fireboat may have a small *rescue boat* on board to carry people in an emergency.

A *fire monitor* produces and sprays foam to extinguish certain kinds of blazes.

A fireboat has several *nozzles*, also known as *deck guns* or *water cannons*, which spray water. Each nozzle can be pointed in any direction.

An extension ladder allows firefighters to access high, hard-to-reach places.

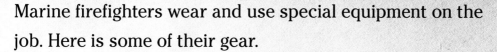

Marine firefighters wear and use special equipment on the job. Here is some of their gear.

The *helmet* is made of strong plastic or leather that will not melt in a fire. Fireproof flaps protect the wearer's neck and ears.

The *face mask* lets firefighters breathe easily by blocking out smoke and heat and providing oxygen from an air tank.

The *air tank* holds about 30 to 60 minutes of air and, in smoky surroundings, allows firefighters to breathe clean air.

The *turnout coat* protects firefighters from heat and fire and is waterproof. It has yellow reflective tape so the wearer is seen more easily in the dark.

Gloves are fire- and water-resistant.

The *fire extinguisher* is filled with carbon dioxide to be used for fires that cannot be extinguished with water.

Fire boots prevent slipping and falling and have thick, protective soles.

Glossary

air filters (AIR FIL-turz) devices that clean air as it passes through them

autonomous (aw-TON-uh-muss) operating by itself

battalion (buh-TAL-yuhn) a large group organized to work together

cabin (KAB-in) a small room on a ship

chainsaws (CHAYN-sawz) gasoline-powered saws

coastal (KOHST-uhl) having to do with land that runs along an ocean or lake

crane (KRANE) a machine with a tall arm

debris (duh-BREE) the scattered pieces of something that has been broken or destroyed

deck (DEK) a platform on the outside of a building

docks (DOKS) landing areas, such as wooden or concrete piers, on the water where a boat may be tied up

emergency (i-MUR-juhn-see) relating to a sudden situation that must be dealt with immediately

extinguished (ek-STING-gwishd) put out a fire

fireboats (FIRE-bohts) boats used to fight fires in or near a body of water

flammable (FLAM-uh-buhl) able to easily catch fire

harbor (HAR-bur) an area of water where ships can safely stay or unload goods

humanoid (HYOO-ma-noyd) resembling a human

intense (in-TENSS) very strong

marinas (muh-REEN-uhz) areas of water that have docks where boats are kept

marine (muh-REEN) having to do with the sea

monitor (MON-uh-tur) to keep track of; to watch carefully

nozzles (NOZ-uhlz) spouts that direct the flow of water from the end of a hose or tube

oil rig (OIL RIG) an offshore platform with equipment used to drill for oil beneath the ocean floor

pier (PEER) a platform that is built over water and is used as a walkway or landing place for boats; a dock

portable (POR-tuh-buhl) able to be carried or easily moved, often by hand

pumps (PUHMPS) machines that force liquids or gases from one place to another

terrorists (TER-ur-ists) individuals or groups that use violence and fear to get what they want

trainees (tray-NEEZ) people who are learning a new skill

units (YOO-nits) groups of workers that are part of a larger group

vessel (VESS-uhl) a ship or large boat

volunteers (vol-uhn-TIHRZ) people who work by choice without pay

Bibliography

Chatterton, Howard. *Marine Fire Fighting for Land-Based Firefighters*. Stillwater, OK: Fire Protection Publications, Oklahoma State University (2001).

Cooper, Geoffrey Lawson. *Floating Fire Engines: A Study of British Fireboats 1835–2005*. Kent, England: Headleys of Ashford (2006).

Harrisson, Frank D. *Shipboard Fire*. Bloomington, IN: AuthorHouse (2005).

Read More

Cutter, Jack. *Phoenix the Fireboat: The True Story*. Signal Hill, CA: ABC Press (2002).

Goldish, Meish. *Firefighters to the Rescue (The Work of Heroes: First Responders in Action)*. New York: Bearport (2012).

Schuh, Mari C. *Fireboats in Action (Pebble Plus: Fighting Fire)*. Mankato, MN: Capstone (2009).

Learn More Online

To learn more about marine firefighters, visit
www.bearportpublishing.com/FireFight!

Index

About the Author

Meish Goldish has written more than 200 books for children. His book *Disabled Dogs* was a Junior Library Guild Selection in 2013. He lives in Brooklyn, New York, not far from where the FDNY fireboat *Bravest* is docked.